A is for Analytics

by Hila Dahan and Jason Thompson · illustrated by Shai Dahan

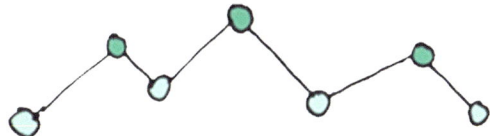

All rights reserved. No part of this book may be reproduced, stored in a retrieval system, or transmitted in any form, by any means, including mechanical, electronic, photocopying, recording, or otherwise, without the prior written consent of the publisher.

Published by 33 Sticks
Words ©2021
Hila Dahan and Jason Thompson
Illustrations ©2021 Shai Dahan

ISBN-978-0-578-32821-8

A is for Analytics
info@aforanalyticsbook.com
www.aforanalyticsbook.com

Hila Dahan and **Jason Thompson** are the owners of 33 Sticks, a boutique analytics agency that advises some of the most recognizable brands in the world on how to use data to create immensely positive customer experiences. Hila is a regular speaker at analytics industry events, while Jason works directly with universities to help shape the next generation of data analysts.

www.33sticks.com

Shai Dahan is an award-winning artist who works with illustrations, sculptures, and murals. He has painted and exhibited internationally and has been featured in numerous publications and television shows, including The New York Times, Huffington Post, BBC and more.

www.shaidahan.com

For Will, Brevin, Halie, Wyatt, Henry, Grace, Ohmri, and Seven

A is for
Analytics

The systematic computational process of understanding data.

Analytics happens when you examine information as you are trying to make a decision. For example, when you try to decide which ice cream flavor to choose at the ice cream shop, you examine the most popular flavors on the list, you think about your favorite flavors from the last time you got ice cream, and you examine what toppings would go best with the flavor you choose... that process is analytics.

B is for
Breakeven

The point at which the number of units you sell covers the cost of developing and producing the units.

The breakeven point is where the money you earned is the same as the money you spent. If you spent $40 to make custom bow ties, and you sell them for $10 each, you will breakeven after you sell your 4th tie.

C is for
Correlation

A mathematical measurement of how linearly related two things are to each other.

For example, in the summer, the temperature goes up.
And when the temperature goes up, so does ice cream sales.
We call this a correlation.

D is for
Data

Facts and statistics collected together for analysis.

Data is everywhere. Look around and you will see data in your everyday life. From how tall you are, to the number of days left until your birthday, to how many donuts you ate last Saturday. It's all data. And you can present data to other people, to help tell a story, make a pitch, or even negotiate something.

DATA

E is for
ETL

Extract - Transform - Load

The procedure of copying data, modifying it to be more useful, and storing it in another location.

When baking a cake, we have to **extract** the ingredients, then combine them in a way that makes sense, then **transform** them into the cake batter, and finally **load** everything into the oven. It's the same with data. We must take different sets of data and find a logical way to connect them and load them to a new location, where we can analyze them.

ETL

Extract

Transform

Load

F is for
Funnel

A method of understanding how the consumer goes through different steps to reach an outcome.

What does a funnel look like? Wide at the top, narrow at the bottom. We use funnels in analysis to visualize a set of steps. For example... of all the people that might visit a website, how many "go down the funnel" and add something to their cart. And then how many of those people "go down the funnel" even further and end up buying something.

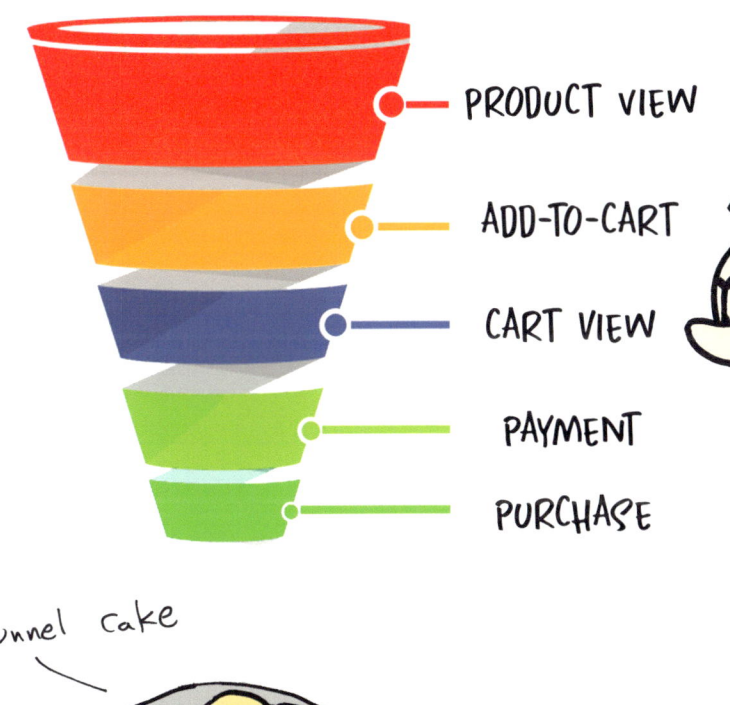

G is for
Graph

A visual representation of data, to help communicate a finding.

A graph is a way we can see data using a picture. For example, you may draw a graph to help your friends visualize how much they like certain types of animals. Of course, llamas would literally be off the charts.

H is for
Histogram

An approximate representation of the distribution of numerical data.

A histogram is a type of chart that helps us understand the frequency of numeric values. We use a histogram when we want to look at buckets of things. For example, our "buckets" could be the different hours of the day, and the height of each bar in the histogram can represent how many people are visiting a website during each hour.

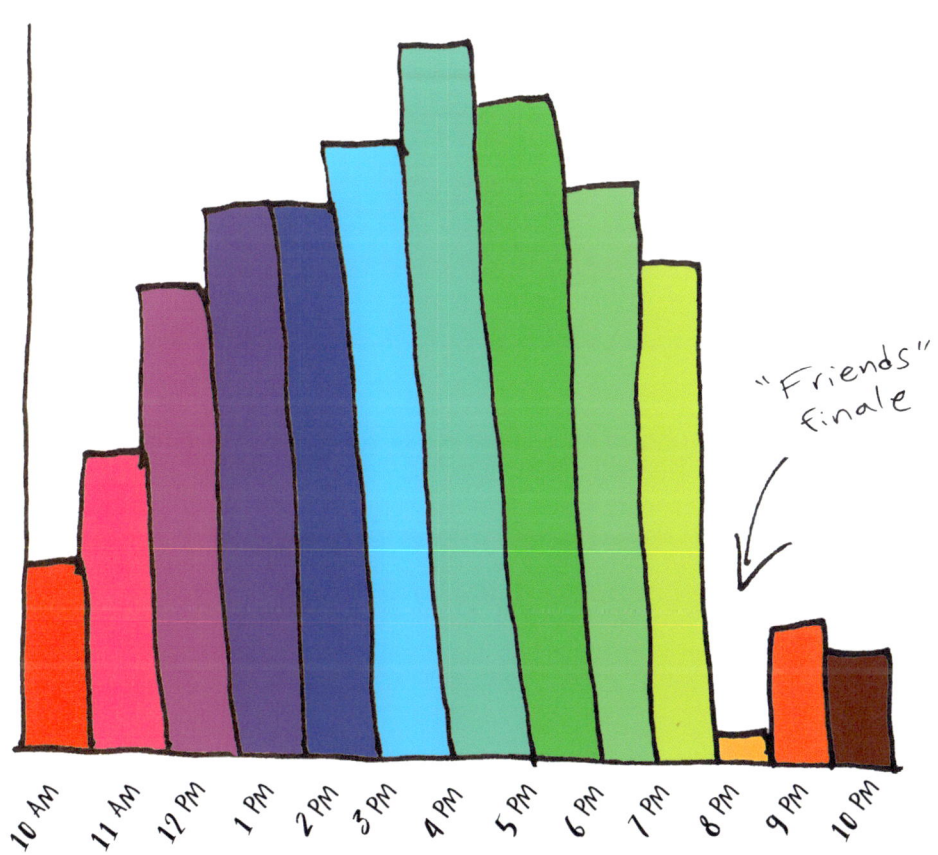

I is for
Impressions

The number of times something was displayed.

Impressions is just a fancy word that typically measures how many ads are displayed to people. For example, it could be the number of times an ad was shown before a video loads, or it could be the number of times that a pop-up message was shown while you were playing a video game. In analytics, we might look at those ad **impressions** and analyze how effective they are.

J is for
JavaScript

A programing language used for web analytics tracking.

JavaScript is a programming language that is often used to capture data about how people use websites. For example, when you visit a website that sells mobile phones, JavaScript is used to capture information about what you purchased, like the product name and price.

JAVASCRIPT

```
transaction.track('ecommerce:transaction, {
'id': '16180',
'item': 'Phone',
'sku': '4109150909',
'category': 'Burners',
'customer last name': 'Pinkman',
'price': '49.99',
'quantity': '1'
});
```

K is for
KPI

Key Performance Indicator.

One of a handful of metrics crucial to the success of a business.

A key performance indicator is a metric that is important to monitor, to make sure things are going well. When you are driving a car, for example, an important metric to monitor is how fast you are going.

L is for
Lifetime Value

How much a person is predicted to spend with a specific store over their entire lifetime.

For example, if you are a loyal customer at a shoe store, that shoe company can probably estimate your "lifetime value" over the next few years. They do this by analyzing your shoe-buying patterns.

M is for
Metrics

The results obtained from measuring something.

Metrics happen when we measure something, like the number of dogs that live in the neighborhood, the number of days until summer break, or how many dentist appointments we've missed.

METRICS

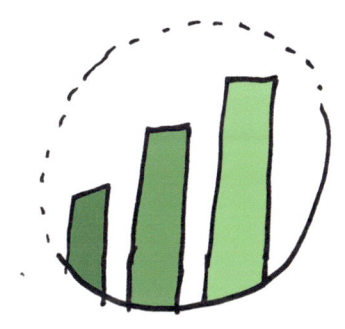

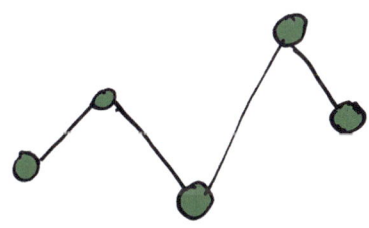

N is for
Normal Distribution

A probability distribution that is symmetric around the mean.

Don't worry. "Mean" is just another word for "Average". And "Average" is a number expressing the central or typical value in a set of data. We use a normal distribution to visualize how close something is to the average. Oh, and when we draw it on a graph it looks like a speed bump.

NORMAL DISTRIBUTION

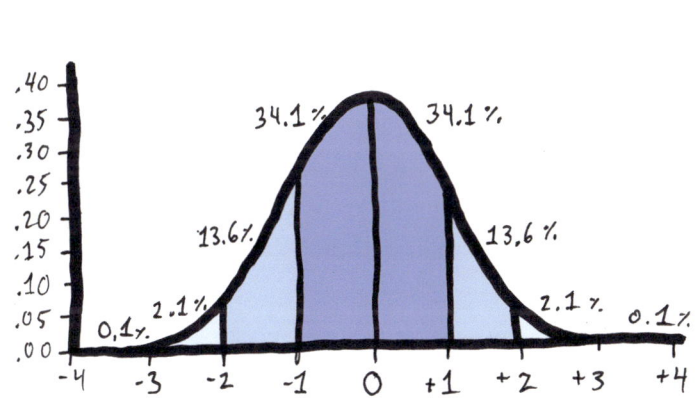

NORMAL DISTRIBUTION

NORMAL SPEED BUMP

O is for
Outlier

A data point that differs significantly from other observations.

An outlier is a data point that is not near all the others, kind of like the pink sheep off doing her own thing.

P is for
P-Value

A measurment of the probability that an observed difference could have occured by random chance.

We use p-value to describe how likely our data is to have occurred by random chance. P-value is often shown as a value between 0 and 1. The smaller the number, the less likely a result is due to random chance. Often, a result of 0.05 or less is said to be "statistically significant".

Q is for
Qualitative Data

Descriptive and conceptual information collected through questionnaires, interviews, or observations.

Qualitative Data is information that is not easily reduced to a number. This type of data is usually collected from focus groups, interviews, and surveys. For example, if someone is asking you a lot of questions about what things you like, they are gathering qualitative data about you.

QUALITATIVE DATA

R is for
Regression

A statistical procedure for estimating the relationship between an **outcome** and the **data that predicts that outcome.**

In analysis, sometimes we want to answer the question of "how closely related is one item to another item". To do that, we use something called regression analysis to visualize that relationship.

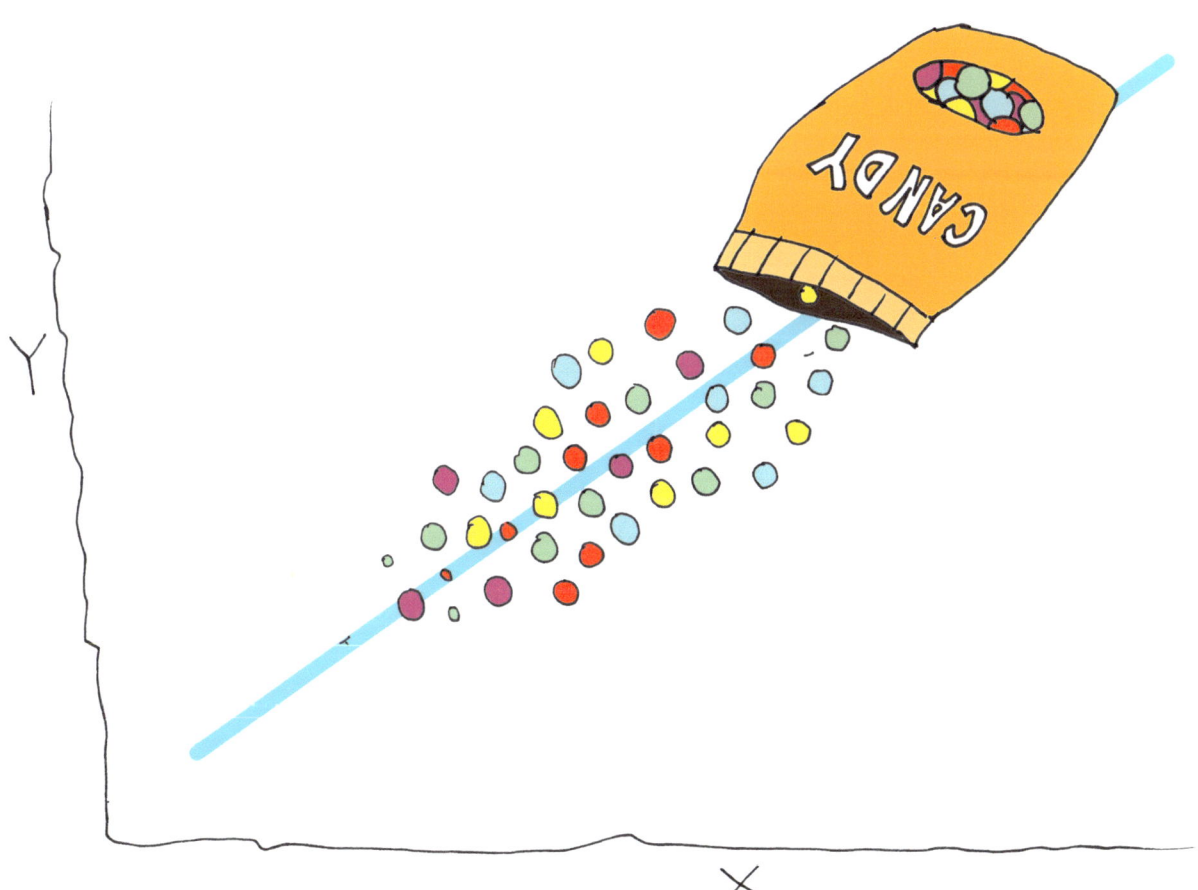

S is for
Segmentation

Dividing a larger population into smaller populations, based on a unique set of characteristics.

We use segmentation when we want to organize things into groups that share similar characteristics. For example, if we want to analyze how much time (on average) kids spend at the skatepark, we might analyze the data by segmenting skateboarders, BMX pros, and scooter riders. This segmentation technique would help us reveal more interesting observations about what's happening at the skatepark.

SEGMENTATION

T is for
Trended Graph

A picture that shows the value of a metric over time.

A trended graph is a way to visualize how data changes over time. Sometimes when the data on a trended graph goes up and down a lot, it kind of looks like a mountain range.

TRENDED GRAPH

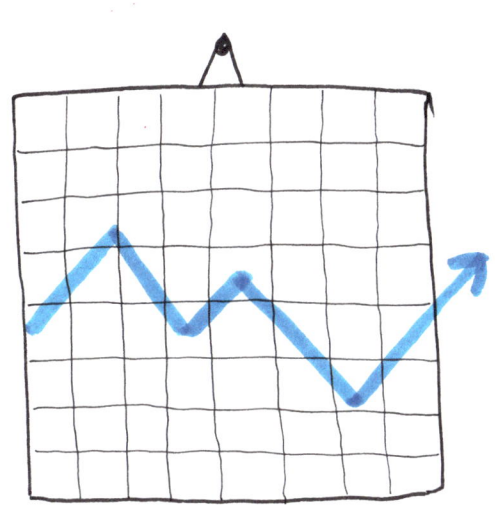

U is for
Unstructured Data

A loose collection of information that is not organized in a pre-defined manner.

If you have random building blocks all over the floor in your room, let's call that "Unstructured Data". To structure the data, we would organize the building blocks into pre-defined groups like color.

UNSTRUCTURED DATA

V is for
Variance

The average of the squared differences from the mean.

We use variance to see how spread out a set of numbers is from their average value. With a large variance, the numbers are really spread out from the average, and the graph looks like a fun gentle rollercoaster ride. But with a small variance, the numbers are very concentrated around the average, and the graph looks like a very steep and scary rollercoaster ride.

VARIANCE

W is for
Week-over-Week

A method of viewing how data changes from one week to the next.

We use a Week-over-Week analysis to see how things change from one week to the next. Maybe last week, we only had one random balloon floating around, but this week, we have 4 balloons. This means that we had a 300% week-over-week increase in balloons.

WEEK OVER WEEK (WOW)

X is for
X-Axis

The line on a graph that runs horizontal, side to side....typically representing an independent variable like **'time of year'**.

The x-axis is used to plot something that causes an effect. Like when the crab walks along the x-axis, it causes the llama to get scared.

Y is for
Y-Axis

The line on a graph that runs vertical, up and down... usually representing a KPI such as **'revenue'**.

The y-axis usually represents a metric showing the scale of an effect. Like when the spider appears, we would measure along the y-axis how high the llama jumps in fear.

Z is for
Z-Score

The number of standard deviations a given data point is away from the mean.

We can use z-scores to compare the length of each llama neck, in comparison to the average neck variation in this specific group of llamas.

The End